A New True Book

YOUR BRAIN AND NERVOUS SYSTEM

By Leslie Jean LeMaster

This "true book" was prepared under the direction of
William H. Wehrmacher, M.D. FACC, FACP
Clinical Professor of Medicine and
Adjunct Professor of Physiology,
Loyola University Stritch School of Medicine,
with the help of his granddaughter Cheryl Sabey

 CHILDRENS PRESS™

CHICAGO

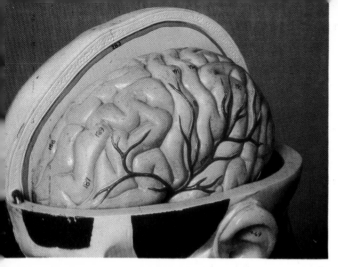

Model of the brain and skull bones

PHOTO CREDITS

©Denoyer-Geppert—16

©EKM-Nepenthe—Tom Ballard, 2, 4 (bottom right), 7 (bottom left), 8 (bottom, two photos), 13 (right), 15 (bottom left), 19, 29, 31, 38; Robert V. Eckert, Jr., 4 (top, bottom left), 41 (right), 42 (2 photos, top); Jean Claude Lejeune, 40; John Maner, 7 (top, left)

©L.V. Bergman & Associates, Inc.—Cover, 15 (bottom right), 25 (bottom)

©Tony Freeman—7 (right), 8 (top, 2 photos), 9, 12 (left), 33, 44 (bottom)

©Reinhard Brucker—13 (left)

©Science Photo Library International—15 (top)

Nawrocki Stock Photo—©Jim Whitmer, 35 (right), 41 (left), 42 (bottom); ©W. S. Nawrocki, 12 (middle and right), 37; ©Phylane Norman—44 (top)

Drawings pages 11, 21, 23, 25, 27, 35 (left) by Phillis Adler

COVER—Brain showing blood vessels

Library of Congress Cataloging in Publication Data

LeMaster, Leslie Jean.
   Your brain and nervous system.

   (A New true book)
   Includes index.
   Summary: A simple presentation of how our brain and nervous system work together to control our body activities and behavior; to enable us to learn, remember, see, smell, speak, and hear; and to feel emotions.
   1. Brain—Juvenile literature. 2. Nervous system—Juvenile literature. [1. Brain. 2. Nervous system]
I. Title.
QP376.L39 1984   612'.82   84-7635
ISBN 0-516-01931-7   AACR2

TABLE OF CONTENTS

HUMANS ARE THE SMARTEST ANIMALS

Everything you learn, feel, do, and remember throughout your life is made possible by certain cells in your body. These cells send messages through your body. They help you move muscles when you want to play ball. They help you remember jokes. They allow you to learn to read and write. They cause you to feel happy or sad. They let you see, smell, speak, and hear. They make your heart beat. They control your breathing and other body activities. These cells make up your nervous system.

The nervous system includes the brain and spinal cord. You are smarter and able to do more things than any other

living animal. That is
because your nervous
system is more developed.
And that is what makes
you human.

Without a nervous system, you would not be able to think, feel, or move. You would not be able to hear, see, talk, breathe, eat, or walk. In fact, you would not be able to do any of the things you do every day. Your life would be about as active as the life of a plant!

THE NERVOUS SYSTEM HAS THREE PARTS

Your nervous system works to control your physical (body) and mental (mind) activities.

It is divided into three parts. One part controls activities like heartbeat and breathing rates. It runs the actions of body parts that are involuntary. This part of your body is not under your control. This part

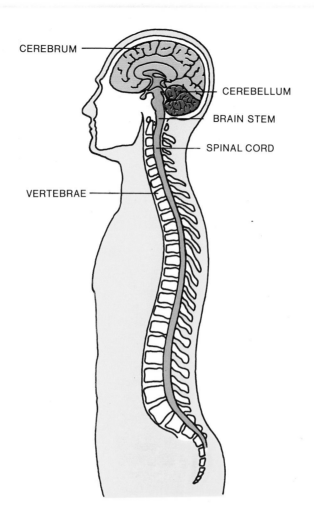

CEREBRUM

CEREBELLUM

BRAIN STEM

SPINAL CORD

VERTEBRAE

includes the lower brain and spinal cord. It is called the autonomic nervous system.

The second part is the
central nervous system. It
includes the brain and
spinal cord. It controls all
thought and organizes
activity. It controls
voluntary actions. These
are movements or activities
controlled by your own
effort.

The last part is the peripheral nervous system. It connects the central nervous system with all parts of the body. It makes you aware of what is around you. This system mainly controls the senses of sight, smell, sound, taste, and touch.

THE BRAIN ORGANIZES EVERYTHING

The brain is made of about three pounds of pinkish-gray tissue. It looks like a cauliflower. It is located in the upper half of the head and contains more than 12 billion nerve cells.

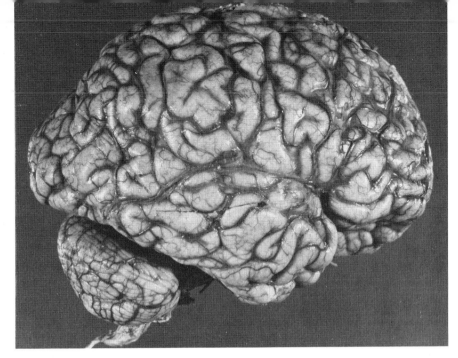

Skull bones surround and protect the brain from injury. The largest part of the brain is the cerebrum. The smaller part, found below the cerebrum, is called the cerebellum. The last part, the brain stem, lies between the cerebrum and the cerebellum. Each part of the brain is important. Each part controls different activities.

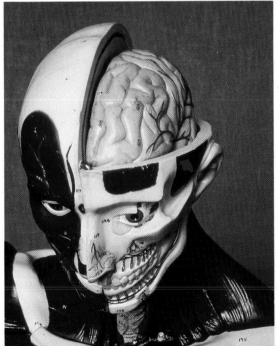

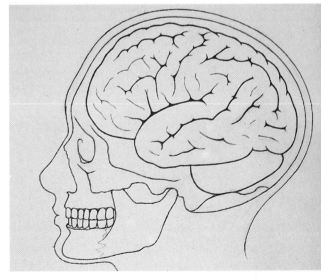

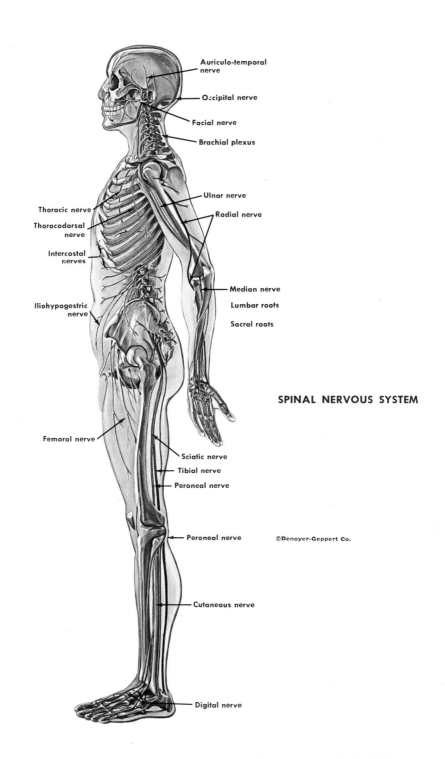

Auriculo-temporal nerve

Occipital nerve

Facial nerve

Brachial plexus

Ulnar nerve

Thoracic nerve

Radial nerve

Thoracodorsal nerve

Intercostal nerves

Median nerve

Lumbar roots

Sacral roots

Iliohypogestric nerve

Femoral nerve

Sciatic nerve

Tibial nerve

Peroneal nerve

SPINAL NERVOUS SYSTEM

Peroneal nerve

©Denoyer-Geppert Co.

Cutaneous nerve

Digital nerve

The brain receives messages through long cells called nerves. These nerves run along the spinal cord and branch out through the body. The brain then sends messages back through the nerves to move the muscles that you want to use.

Suppose you want to turn on a radio. This looks easy. Yet many voluntary muscles must be used to do this simple activity.

Voluntary muscles are muscles you can move by your own effort.

First you have to turn your head and move your eyes to see the radio. Then you must walk over to the radio. Next you must grasp the knob, then turn it. In order to do this, your voluntary muscles must work in the right order. It would be useless to try to grasp the radio knob before you walk over

to it. These movements of
your muscles are
controlled by your brain.

The brain is truly an
amazing organ. Think about
the complicated things it
can do!

THE PARTS
OF YOUR BRAIN

The brain has three main sections. The largest section is called the cerebrum. The second largest is the cerebellum. And the smallest is the brain stem. Each works to control different activities.

The cerebrum is the wrinkled upper part of the brain. It is divided into two halves of nerve tissue. The cerebrum controls all

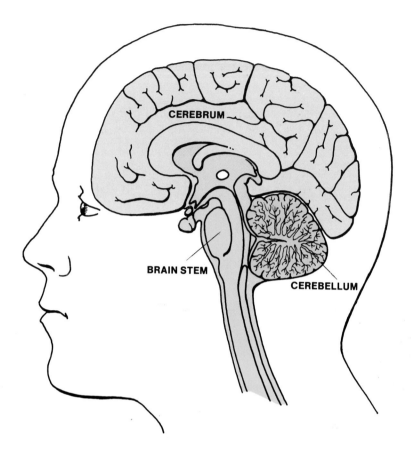

voluntary muscles. It is the
center that controls
thinking, memory, sensations,
and emotions.

The cerebellum lies
under the back of the

cerebrum. This section is also divided into two halves. The cerebellum allows you to learn habits and develop motor (movement) skills. It causes the voluntary muscles used in activities to work in the right order. The cerebellum also controls your sense of balance. If your cerebellum were injured, you would feel dizzy and wobbly.

The brain stem lies between the cerebrum,

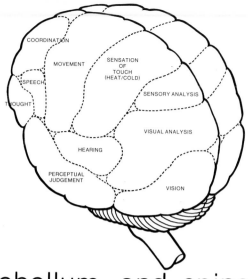

cerebellum, and spinal cord. This section controls the involuntary muscles of the body. It regulates heartbeat rate, breathing rate, blood circulation, and digestion. It also controls many other involuntary activities. Injury to this area can cause these activities to stop.

YOUR SPINAL CORD

The spinal cord is a long cord made of nerve cells. It runs from the brain all the way down the middle of the back. The nerves in the spinal cord carry messages, or impulses, to and from the brain.

Nerve cells are also called neurons. There are millions of neurons in the

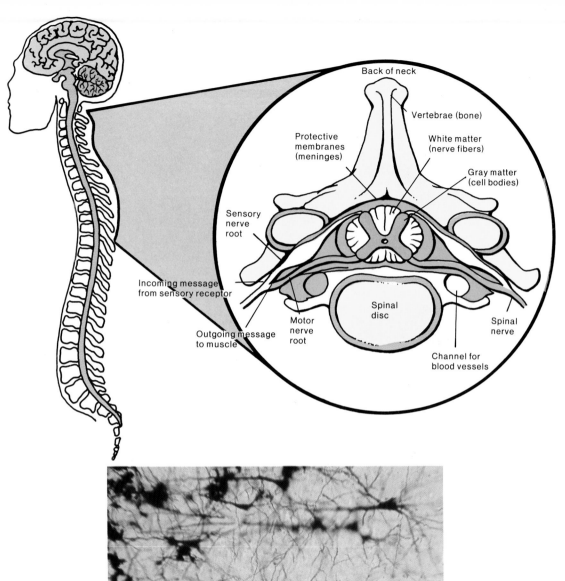

Back of neck

Vertebrae (bone)

Protective
membranes
(meninges)

White matter
(nerve fibers)

Gray matter
(cell bodies)

Sensory
nerve
root

Incoming message
from sensory receptor

Spinal
disc

Motor
nerve
root

Spinal
nerve

Outgoing message
to muscle

Channel for
blood vessels

Nerve cells
in the brain
receive and send
messages.

body. Like other cells, each neuron has a cell body with branches that go out in all directions. These thin branches are called dendrites. They send messages to the cell body.

Each neuron also has a nerve fiber that goes out from the cell body. This fiber is called an axon. Some axons are very short, and some are very long. They carry messages away from cell bodies. A bunch

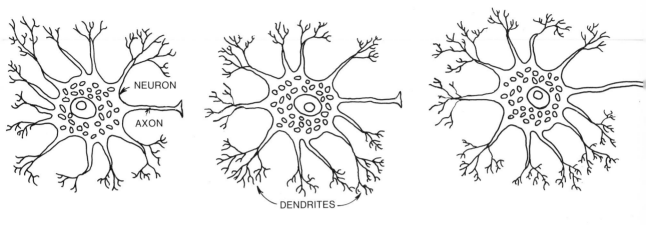

of neurons make up nerve
tissue.

Neurons are arranged so
that the axon of one
neuron lies near the
dendrite of another.
Between the two neurons
is a gap. When a message
moves along a nerve, the
axon carries the message

away from its cell body.
The message jumps over
the gap to the dendrite of
the next neuron. The
dendrite then carries the
message to its cell body.
The axon of that cell body
then carries the message
over the gap to the next
neuron. In this way, the
message, or impulse, is
carried from cell to cell
through the body.

Pulling your hand away from a hot object is an automatic or reflex action.

REFLEX ACTIONS PROTECT YOU

Suppose you touch something hot. Before you feel pain, your nerves send a message to your spinal cord. These nerves make you quickly move your hand away. You do not even have time to think about it. You act automatically. This automatic action is called a reflex action. Then the message is carried from your spinal cord to your brain, where you feel it as pain.

Reflex actions help protect your body from harm. If you had to decide what to do when something is about to hurt

Putting your arms out to break a fall is a reflex action.

you, you might become frightened and make the wrong move. The automatic action of reflexes makes your body move correctly and quickly. This helps prevent or lessen the danger facing you.

THE BRAIN AND SPINAL CORD WORK TOGETHER

Suppose you get a mosquito bite on your arm. Nerves from your arm send a message up through your spinal cord to your brain. This message tells your brain that your arm is itching. Your brain then

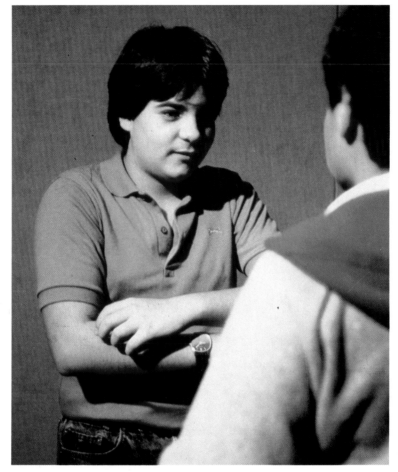

Your brain receives and sends messages through the spinal cord.

sends a message down through the spinal cord to your hand. This message tells your hand to scratch the mosquito bite.

WHY MOST PEOPLE ARE RIGHT-HANDED

Most people are right-handed, but some are left-handed.

The brain has a right half and a left half. The right half of the brain controls the muscles on the left side of the body. And the left half of the brain controls the right side of the body.

In most people, the left half of the brain is more

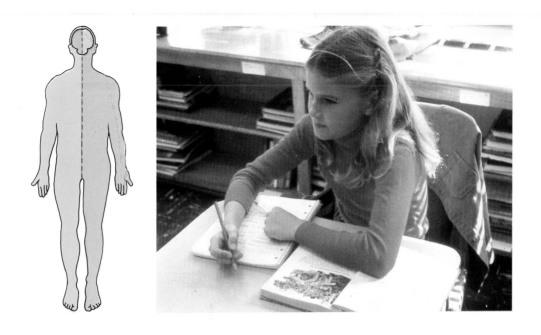

powerful or dominant than the right side. They have better control of the movements on the right sides of their bodies. And so they are better able to do things with their right hands. These people are said to be right-handed.

BRAIN CELLS DIE

The brain has billions of nerve cells. But after the age of eighteen about one thousand cells die every day. These dead nerve cells are not replaced 'with new cells.

Don't worry that your brain will run out of cells. If your brain lost one thousand cells per day, it would take more than 100,000 years for it to run out of cells.

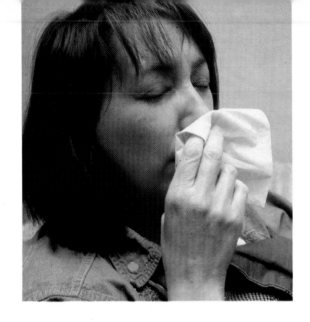

SNEEZING IS A REFLEX ACT

Sneezing is a reflex action of the body to protect itself. You cannot control it.

Sneezing is caused by an irritation of nerve endings in the nose. The irritation can come from bacteria or

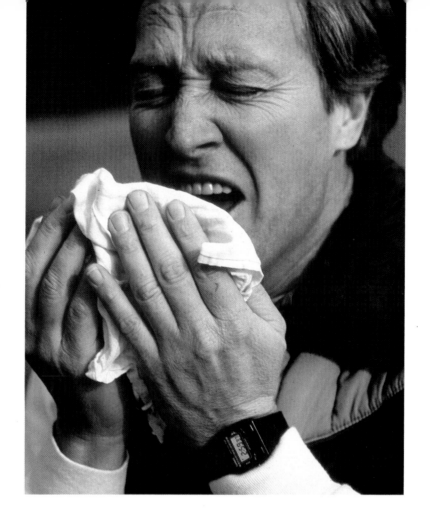

dust in the air that you breathe into your nose.

Sneezing is the body's way of getting rid of the irritating material.

YOU ARE SMARTER
THAN A COMPUTER

You are smarter than a computer because you have a brain. A computer can only do what someone programs it to do. It cannot think, experience, or feel things. But once a computer is programmed,

Only humans can think.

it works faster than a human brain. In a few minutes it can solve a problem that would take a person a long time to figure out.

THE BODY NEEDS REST

Did you ever wonder why you feel tired at the end of the day?

All day long, muscles work to move all parts of your body. When muscles

work, they produce a chemical. The body also produces chemicals when muscles are active. Blood carries the chemicals through the body. At the end of the day, these chemicals build up or accumulate in the body and cause it to feel tired. To get rid of the tired feeling, you go to sleep.

Sleep allows the nerve cells in your body to rest and repair themselves.

In the brain, there is an area called a sleep center. Activity of nerves and muscles sends a chemical into the blood. This chemical causes the sleep center to work. And so you get sleepy.

Sleep allows your body cells to rest and to repair. Sleep is needed to restore energy to your body and your brain.

WORDS YOU SHOULD KNOW

accumulate(a • KYOOM • u • late) — to pile up or increase in quantity

automatic(aw • toe • MAT • ick) — moving or acting by itself

communicate(ka • MU • nih • kate) — to send or exchange information from one location to another

complicated(KOM • plih • kay • ted) — difficult or not easy to do

dominant(DOM • in • nant) — ruling or controlling

impulse(IM • puls) — the passage of activity through a nerve

involuntary(in • VOL • un • ter • ee) — occurring without choice or control

irritation(ear • rih • TAY • shun) — an annoyance or sensitivity

muscle(MUS • sul) — a tissue that works to produce body movements

nerve(NURV) — fiber that sends impulses between the brain or spinal cord and other parts of the body

reflex(REE • fleks) — an involuntary body movement in response to a stimulus or stimulation of that body part

stimulus(STIM • u • lus) — something that excites a part of the body to cause a response

tissue(TISH • u) — a group of the same kind of cells that work together to do a certain job

voluntary(VOL • un • ter • ee) — occurring by choice or by conscious effort

INDEX

About the author

Leslie Jean LeMaster received a Bachelor of Arts Degree in Psychology and has taken postgraduate courses in Clinical and Physiological Psychology. She has worked in the Child Guidance Clinic at Children's Hospital in Northern California, helping parents and children with behavioral problems to interrelate. Ms. LeMaster has completed a manuscript on an introduction to the human anatomy for middle grade-level children. She has written another book in the New True Book Series titled Your Heart and Blood published by Childrens Press. Ms. LeMaster currently owns and operates her own business in Irvine, California, and is the mother of a nine-year-old daughter.